Mary Elitch Long
First Lady of Fun

Mary Elitch Long
First Lady of Fun

A NOW YOU KNOW BIO

Number Nine in the Series

Debra B. Faulkner

Filter Press, LLC

Palmer Lake, Colorado

To James, who sustains my sense of wonder.

Cover image courtesy Denver Public Library, Western History Collection.

ISBN: 978-0-86541-094-7
Library of Congress Control Number: 2008925735
Copyright © 2008 Debra B. Faulkner

Mary Elitch Long: First Lady of Fun
Published by
Filter Press, LLC, P.O. Box 95, Palmer Lake, Colorado 80133
719.481.2420 • *info@filterpressbooks.com*

Printed in the United States of America

Contents

Courtesy of Betty Lynne Hull

What do you want to do when you grow up? Adults ask all children the same question. One young lady wanted to do the same things when she grew up that she did as a little girl. Mary Elitch wanted to have fun. She wanted to surround herself with flowers and animals. She wanted excitement and entertainment.

Mary imagined that people of all ages enjoyed the same things she did. As an adult, Mary found a way to share her joys with others. She became the first woman in the world to own and run a zoo. Her beautiful gardens were also a popular picnic grounds and **amusement park**. Visitors came from everywhere to enjoy rides on her **carousel** and roller coaster, too. And no summer's day was complete without a show at Mary's famous theater in the gardens.

Mary's Elitch Gardens set the scene for countless happy memories. Despite loss and tragedies in her personal life, Mary created beauty, romance, and magical times for all in her famous Denver, Colorado, amusement park.

*This poster advertising the 1890 opening of the Gardens
included founder John Elitch Jr.'s portrait.*

1 Following Her Heart

Throughout her long life, Mary Elitch Long remained a child at heart. She never lost her sense of wonder.

Mary spoke little of her early years. "Just say the fairies landed me in the Hauck family one fine May morning," she would laugh. "That's enough for that part of me." Mary Elizabeth Hauck was born in Philadelphia, Pennsylvania, on May 10, 1856. She was the eldest of six children. Her family called her "Lydia." Little Mary was nearly three when her family moved to a California farm. She grew up outside of the booming city of San Francisco. She was a tenderhearted child with a ready smile. During the school year, she lived at a **convent** school run by Roman Catholic nuns.

Mary Hauck never liked her last name. While she was still in her teens, she got the chance to change it.

John Elitch Jr. came into Mary's life when she was just 16. They met at church. The twenty-two-year-old athlete and actor was handsome and dashing. John had dark curly hair and deep blue eyes. He swept Mary off her feet. Her parents thought she was too young to marry. But she always followed her heart. She and John eloped. They ran away together to San Jose, California, and wed in 1872.

John and Mary had been married for eight years when they decided to move to Colorado. The four-year-old state held the promise of adventure. By then, John had experience in the restaurant business. He and Mary opened a cafe in Durango. Encouraged by its success, they headed for the big city of Denver in 1882. Four years later, they opened a restaurant at 1561 Arapahoe Street. They called it the Elitch Palace Dining Room.

The restaurant quickly became a favorite with visitors and locals alike. Its customers included some of the most famous and powerful people in Denver. Newspaper editors, writers, actors, politicians, and businessmen all enjoyed dining at the Elitch Palace. Along with some of these important people, John helped to start the Denver Athletic Club. The club provided a gym and exercise areas for its sports-minded members.

Mary Hauck was sixteen when she eloped with John Elitch Jr.

John and Mary Elitch were happily married for nineteen years.

When she wasn't helping John at the restaurant, Mary painted pictures. She served as president of the Denver Art Club. She adopted stray dogs and cats, whether there was room for them in their little rented house or not.

As business at the restaurant improved, John and Mary were able to buy a larger place. The 16-acre Chilcott Farm lay five miles northwest of Denver in an area called the Highlands. The property included a farmhouse, apple and cherry orchards, and many beautiful cottonwood trees. The Elitches soon added vegetable gardens. Now they could grow their own fruits and vegetables for the restaurant.

Mary planted flowers and bushes along pathways that wound through the orchards. Their farm became a wonderfully pleasant place to spend time. They thought it seemed a shame to keep it all to themselves. What if we opened our gardens to the public? they wondered. Streetcar tracks had recently reached the corner of their property. The little steam train could bring people from the city right to the gate.

The Elitches had more than just plants to share with visitors. Circus owner P. T. Barnum gave John and Mary baby animals to care for. Their friend Adam Forepaugh shopped around for other animals. Before long, the Elitches had quite a **menagerie** of bears, lion cubs, and monkeys on their property. They even had an ostrich. There were no zoos between Chicago and the West Coast at the time. Coloradans would gladly pay to see these unusual animals up close.

John built a log entrance gate to their property at the corner of 38th and Tennyson Streets. On May 1, 1890, Elitch's Zoological Gardens opened for business. But that morning, John and Mary looked out their window at the pouring rain. They wondered if anyone would come. They needn't have worried.

Mary remembered, "The little train engine came to a stop at the gates. It seemed to pant in relief while its enormous crowd of passengers poured out of its cars. How those people rushed the gates! It certainly looked as if the entire population of Denver had accepted our invitation."

One treat for children visiting Elitch Gardens was a ride through the park in a goat cart.

Elitch's opened with a fanfare of trumpets. Denver mayor Wolfe Londoner gave a welcome speech. P. T. Barnum brought the famous midget Tom Thumb and his tiny wife. Many of John's friends from the theater came, some of them famous stars. People came in wagons, in carriages, and on bicycles, ignoring the rain.

It was a special place from the very beginning. Park benches and picnic tables allowed guests to enjoy the lovely flower beds and fountains. Brass bands entertained from the **gazebo** stage. The Gardens also hosted friendly afternoon baseball games.

Mary planned playgrounds especially for children. Swings, slides, and teeter-totters kept them busy while their parents relaxed. Pony rides and goat cart rides were special treats.

Elitch's Orchard Café served delicious lunches to those who came without picnic baskets. Nearby, a soda fountain booth sold refreshing beverages. A confectionary shop offered tempting sweets and desserts.

Visitors also enjoyed **vaudeville** shows put on by John and his friends. The shows included comedians, singers, dancers, acrobats, athletes, and musicians. The stage was outdoors under a large tent. People who could not get seats stood under big shade trees to watch the performances.

Elitch's gates closed for the season on Labor Day. The first summer was a huge success. It was a good thing, because John had sold their restaurant. There was no turning back for the Elitches now. The park was the fulfillment of their dreams.

John used the money they made to take his acting group on tour in California that winter. While performing in San Francisco, John caught pneumonia. The serious lung infection made it difficult to breathe. His illness quickly grew worse. Mary rushed to be by John's side. Three weeks later on March 10, 1891, he died. The love of her life was suddenly gone. Mary was now a 34-year-old **widow**.

How could she go on without him? Mary could not imagine. Returning to Denver, she cried and cried. Her heart was broken. What was she to do now? John had always made the decisions. She felt lost.

Gradually, the springtime beauty of the gardens began to comfort her. Mary felt the healing power of nature. She fixed flowerpots, planted seeds, and wandered through the blossoming orchards. She recalled how much the gardens and the park had meant to John. Taking care of them was the best way to keep his memory alive.

Mary tended her gardens and her animals with renewed purpose. "While the birds were outlining their summer plans in the trees above me, I told myself, as this was to be my life work, I might as well begin," Mary later recalled. Summer was right around the corner. She had much to do before thousands of visitors once again lined up at her gate.

Elitch Gardens' popular picnic grounds were shaded by apple, cherry, and cottonwood trees.

Postcard courtesy of Leona L. Gustafson

2 Mary's Menagerie

Imagine having a bear for a pet. Or a lion cub sleeping in your bed. Or a monkey interrupting your chores. Mary Elitch didn't have to imagine. She shared her life with unusual animals every day. Mary loved animals, and after her husband died, her animals became even more important to her. They became her family.

Mary's menagerie grew and changed over the years that she ran Denver's first zoo. Bears, lion cubs, ostriches, camels, water buffalo, elephants, kangaroos, and peacocks made themselves at home in Elitch's Gardens. Mary welcomed them all as her honored guests.

She raised many of the animals from babies. They were used to having her in their cages and **enclosures**. They trusted her.

Mary raised several lion cubs by hand. They had been taken away from their mothers because the circus couldn't use them. She bottle-fed them as babies. She cared for them until they grew too big to play with safely. When the lions were grown, they were given to other zoos. Sending her young lions to faraway zoos must have felt like sending children off to college.

A lion cub named Gladys was one of many zoo babies bottle-fed and lovingly cared for by Mary

She had full-grown lions, too. Rex was a handsome male. He was the model for the stone lion sculptures at the entrance to the Chicago Art Institute. Another grown male, Ed, was Mary's favorite lion. When he died, she had his coat made into a rug for her cottage. That way, she could still see him every day.

The animals that had been circus performers knew lots of tricks. Sam the bear was a splendid dancer. For years, he and Mary delighted crowds in the gardens by waltzing together beautifully.

A naughty monkey named Dude was a bit of a troublemaker. In those days, ladies wore fancy hats to the park. When a lady offered Dude peanuts, he might snatch the hat right off her head! The thief then scampered up a tree with his prize. He'd quickly pluck the hat clean of flowers and feathers and shred them. Dude was often locked up on monkey "time out" for this bad habit.

Mary taught some of her animal friends new tricks. She trained a clever ostrich to pull a sulky, a little rubber-tired two-wheeled cart. Mrs. Elitch sped around the gardens in her ostrich-powered vehicle. Ostriches are surprisingly fast and strong! Some members of Mary's menagerie helped out with jobs around the grounds. An elephant named Jess cleared big tree stumps. Sometimes he even moved small buildings.

Elitch's Zoo was also home to many Colorado animals. Deer, elk, and even rattlesnakes were part of the menagerie. Most kinds of snakes in the snake pit were harmless. But they could still cause excitement. Once, their keeper forgot to feed them. The hungry reptiles smelled the nearby picnics. They climbed up the steep walls and out of their pit. Snakes slithered onto the shoulders and into the laps of unsuspecting diners leaning against the enclosure. Panicked picnickers attacked the invading snakes. Zookeepers had to rush to the reptiles' rescue.

Elitch's also had seals. Mary bought the first one from a sea captain. That night, she was awakened by strange cries and barks.

Dressing quickly, for I was quite used to being called upon to quiet my animals when they became frightened in the night, I hurried to the scene of disturbance and discovered I had purchased two seals instead of one! The mother was voicing her delight over the arrival of her baby, and the baby was protesting the chilliness of the world into which it had just entered.

The baby was the first seal to be born in a zoo. Elitch's held a contest to name the mother and the new baby seal. The contest winners suggested *Celia* for the mother and *Cellina* for her baby.

Mary wrote a series of animal studies booklets for children. She handed them out for free to teach children about the zoo creatures. These booklets described how the animals lived in the wild. They explained what they ate and their other habits. Mary's booklets helped the children who visited Elitch's understand and appreciate animal behavior.

"I do not dislike any animal," Mary said. "I like least hyenas, coyotes, and wolves." She liked lions, deer, and antelope best. "My lions when young follow me about the grounds and run about the house like pups."

Mary's favorite pet bears were named Sam and Dewey. Each evening as the park prepared to close, they

Know More!

What is your favorite zoo animal? Use books and magazines, the Internet, and television to learn more about the animal. Then write an Animal Study booklet like Mary's. Include the answers to these questions:

What sort of home does your animal need in a zoo?

What will you feed your animal?

Is it safe for your animal to interact with humans?

Decorate the cover of your Animal Study with a picture of you and the animal.

Mary had a unique way of getting around the Gardens. She trained an ostrich to pull a light-weight cart.

were let out of the bear pit. Two bears lumbering past on their way to Mary's cottage for dinner was a startling sight. It was usually enough to clear the Gardens of its late-day visitors.

One day Mary arrived home to find an uninvited bear in her little cottage. Daisy had escaped the pit. The big bear was sitting on the kitchen counter. Daisy had figured out how the faucet worked and was splashing water all over the place. When she saw Mary, Daisy leapt down and lunged at her. Mary raced to the door to escape. But Daisy was too quick. Before Mary knew it, the bear had her pinned against the dining room sideboard, a piece of furniture for displaying china.

Mary was in a dangerous spot. Most people would have panicked. Mary kept her head and thought fast. She reached for the sugar bowl on the shelf behind her. She knew Daisy couldn't resist the sweet treat. Mary slowly set the bowl on the floor and pushed it away.

Mary was always kind to her zoo animals. She had a very special relationship that gave her the confidence to visit Jim the bear in the bear pit.

James   George   Richard   Arthur   Russell   Earl   Norman   Karl
  Donald   Walter   Vincent   Roger   Sherman   Paul   Allison   Tommie
    Howard   Billie   Hughsey   Leland   Charles   Eugene   Sidney ― Leslie

Mrs. Elitch and Her Pet Kids.

Rudy   Francis   Genevieve   Elizabeth   Myra   Lillian   Maud   Gladys
  Anna   Virginia   Hannah   Cornelia   Ethelyn   Betty   Gertrude   Nellie
    Nancy Laffin   Sarah   Emily   Josephine   Helen   Edna   Kathrin   Mildred

Mary named each of Elitch's many baby animals. These are the names she gave to the zoo's goats. Do any of the kids have your name?

From Experiences of the Only Woman ... to Manage a Zoo. Courtesy, Denver Public Library

Daisy had to take her big paws off Mary's shoulders to reach it.

While the bear lapped up the sugar, Mary made a break for the door. In a flash, she slammed it shut. She called for the keeper, who took Daisy back to the pit. It had been a close call for Mary. Her presence of mind—and the bear's sweet tooth—probably saved her life.

Mary's animal family was a big part of the second season success of Elitch's Gardens and Zoological Park.

Postcard courtesy of Leona L. Gustafson

Ladies wore breezy gauze dresses and fancy hats to summer matinee performances at Elitch's Theatre. Here they gather at the Gardens' original log entrance gate.

Mary had to learn about business fast. At that time, she was the only woman in the world running a zoo. Mary made good choices and good money. She sold **shares** of the park business to **investors**. Within three years, she was able to buy back all the shares of the Gardens.

Mary advertised the Gardens in newspapers, on posters, and on postcards. One early newspaper ad invited visitors to "Come see the bears stand up and beg for peanuts, the monkeys slide down their toboggan slide…And the baby bears—why, they're a whole zoological park in themselves! Come gaze in wonder at Mac, the largest lion in captivity."

The best advertising for Elitch's was word-of-mouth. People who came out to enjoy the Gardens told their friends and family what a wonderful time they'd had. More and more visitors found their way there each season. People came not only from Denver, but also from all over the state. Many brought relatives from other states or other countries. Elitch's **reputation** spread far and wide.

When the Denver Zoo opened in City Park in 1896, Mary donated many of her animals to the new **attraction.** She kept a few special pets and the most interesting animals for the enjoyment of her visitors. Animals continued to keep her company in the Gardens for most of her life.

By the late 1890s, Elitch's Gardens was moving beyond the zoo business. Mary busied herself with planning new surprises to delight visitors. She was about to shift her main efforts in a new direction.

3 The Next Stage

Mary had never seen a play before she married John. Shortly after their wedding, John took her to see *The Streets of New York*. From the moment the curtain rose, Mary was enchanted by the theater.

Before he died, John had designed a theater for the Gardens. The eight-sided building had an unusual domed roof. It was modeled after the Globe, a famous historic theater in London, England, where Shakespeare's plays had been performed.

Construction of the theater had just begun when Elitch's opened for its first season. By the second summer, it was complete. Mary continued to present vaudeville acts for the first few seasons. Then she added performances of light opera. The Playhouse in the Gardens was one of the park's most popular attractions.

Mary wanted it to be first class. She brought important plays and famous actors to Denver. Many of John's close friends from the entertainment world were a great help to Mary. One of them, Charles Schilling, married her younger sister, Anna Hauck.

Elitch's theater made history in 1896. It showed the first moving pictures ever seen in the American West. Inventor Thomas Edison's "Vitascope" projected images onto a large screen. It was the great-granddaddy of today's movies.

Electric lights were another Edison invention used at Elitch's. They were kept lighted by the Garden's own power plant. The glowing globes turned night into day. They also attracted moths and other flying insects. Mary felt sorry for the fragile creatures that seemed to mistake the hot bulbs for the moon. She wrote a children's story about the moths that died in the lights entitled *The Moth and the Moon*.

Mary added more **landscaping** and stone zoo buildings. She also opened a penny **arcade**. Game booths offered ring toss and target shooting. Skillful—and lucky—players won stuffed animals and other prizes.

In 1897, Elitch Gardens launched its summer stock theater in the Playhouse in the Gardens. The theater company reused its "stock" stage sets and costumes in production after production. The ten-week season presented ten different plays. Directed by George Edeson, *A Bachelor's Romance, Fool of Fortune,* and *The Rajah* were among the plays that delighted audiences.

Famous actor James O'Neill honored a promise to his late friend, John Elitch Jr. O'Neill appeared as the theater's first leading man. O'Neill's son, Eugene, later became one of America's most famous **playwrights.**

The Elitch Gardens Orchestra provided music for the theatrical performances. Led by Rafaello Carvello, this was Denver's first symphony orchestra. Maestro

John Elitch Jr. designed the eight-sided, green and white Playhouse in the Gardens, photographed here in 1923.

Carvello's Friday afternoon outdoor concerts were not to be missed. Ladies brought their knitting, sewing, or books, as well as their babies to the concerts.

Not all the drama at Elitch's was onstage. Local daredevil Ivy Baldwin thrilled visitors with his gas-filled balloon. It was 65-feet around. Tied to the ground, it rose a dizzying 1,500 feet into the air. On the Fourth of July, Baldwin dangled from the balloon basket by a rope and lit fireworks strapped to his back! His death-defying feats thrilled Elitch crowds for ten summers.

Dr. Carver's diving horses offered another jaw-dropping attraction at Elitch's Gardens in 1905. The star horses, Powderface and Cupid, bravely leapt from atop a 35-foot wooden tower into a deep pool of water!

When the Gardens closed each season, Mary spent the winter months in New York City or San Francisco. These big cities were famous for their theater. Mary attended all the new plays, looking for shows that Denver audiences would enjoy. She also looked for the best actors and actresses for her theater. She offered performers as much money as they made in the larger cities.

Elitch's theater was very popular. Audiences often overflowed the indoor seating. When that happened, one wall of the theater was opened out. Then people could stand under the stars to watch the performances.

Brave visitors to Elitch's floated high above the treetops in the basket of the aeroballoon ride. The "Ascension" sign kept count of how many times the balloon went up.

The stage could also be expanded outdoors for forest scenes beneath real trees.

In 1899, Mary hired Thomas D. Long to manage the playhouse. He had experience managing a Denver drug store that belonged to his first wife's father. Long had been widowed twice when he met Mary. He understood the pain of losing a loving partner, just as Mary did.

Long became more than just an assistant to Mary. And in time, he became much more than a friend. In November 1900, Mary became Mrs. Thomas Long. Their small wedding was held at the Gardens cottage. Reporting on the marriage, the *Denver Times* said of Mary: "Perhaps nowhere in the city of Denver is to be found a more honestly popular woman...public spirited in the broadest sense." The story described Thomas as having "a uniform courtesy and a naturally magnetic personality."

The newlyweds set off on a trip around the world. They traveled for six months. Upon their return, a reporter from the *Denver Republican* interviewed Mary about their adventures. "Sat on the floor in a Japanese theater and climbed Vesuvius" the headlines said. "Rode elephants in India, camels in Egypt, but like Denver trolley cars best."

"Oh dear! We have been so far and we have seen so much," exclaimed Mrs. Long, "I feel like a boy who has been running a race and is so completely out of breath that he cannot tell about it."

Back home at the Gardens, "all the mountain lions and bears yesterday smiled their best welcome," the *Republican* reported Mary as saying. But Mary's favorite bear, Dewey, was not there to greet her. He had missed her terribly. Somehow he got out of the bear pit one evening while she was gone. He broke a window trying to get into Mary's cottage. The bear cut himself on the broken glass. Before anyone found him, the poor animal bled to death. Mary was heartsick at the news. Dewey had been a dear friend.

The couple turned their attention to remodeling Elitch's theater. They made it bigger and better than ever. An actress friend of Mary's, Margaret Fealy, started the Elitch School of Drama and Theater.

One early star at Elitch's was 11 years old when she first appeared on the stage. Antoinette Perry was a Denver girl. She acted with her father, Frederick. Antoinette was called "Tony" for short. She grew up to be a famous producer of plays on Broadway in New York City. Broadway's highest honors, the Tony Awards, presented each year are named for her.

The Playhouse in the Gardens' reputation grew in the early 1900s. Many famous and soon-to-be-famous actors and actresses performed there. By far the most famous actress of the day was Sarah Bernhardt. "The Divine Miss Sarah" might never have appeared at Elitch's had it not been for a natural disaster. She was supposed to perform in San Francisco in the summer of 1906. But the theater was destroyed by a terrible earthquake and fire. Suddenly without a place to perform, the actress accepted Elitch's invitation.

Miss Bernhardt appeared for one day only—but what a day! She played the starring role in *Camille* for the afternoon **matinee.** That evening, she played a completely different role as a magical **sorceress** in *La Sorciere.* Her moving performances left Denver audiences awestruck.

One day, a boy of twelve came around begging for a job. He was willing to do anything for free theater tickets. The janitor put him to work scrubbing the stage. Years later, that same Denver boy returned to the theater as a leading man. Douglas Fairbanks had become a Hollywood movie star. This time, nobody handed him a scrub brush.

Elitch Gardens and Theater became a summer tradition. People adored Mary for creating a place for all to enjoy. *Denver Post* drama critic Frank White was the first to call her the "Lady of the Gardens." It seemed that the dream might go on forever. Sadly, some rude awakenings lay ahead for Mary Elitch Long.

4 Growing Mary's Garden

Mary and Thomas Long made more improvements to the gardens. Their travels had given them lots of ideas. Amusement parks were popular everywhere. Concerts and plays, animals and playgrounds were no longer enough. The big new attractions were rides.

At the famous Luna Park in New York, Mary had tried out a thrilling invention. The Figure 8 Toboggan Coaster ride was a train of two-seater cars. It snaked up steep hills. It plummeted down sheer drops and swooped along tracks that twisted every which way. When the ride was over, Mary caught her breath. She straightened her hat and pinned it on tighter. "Let's do it again!" she cried excitedly. By 1904, Elitch's had its own Figure 8 Roller Coaster.

The Longs also ordered a carousel from the Philadelphia Toboggan Company. It was a one-of-a-kind work of art. Wooden horses alone wouldn't do for Elitch's. The ride's forty-six animals included giraffes, zebras, bears, and lions. "Miss Mary's carousel" even had a hippocampus, part horse and part fish – always a very popular mount.

The carousel animals were hand-carved and decorated in amazing detail. The deer had real antlers. The horses' tails were actual horsehair. The wooden animals raced around the carousel counterclockwise. In the center, the Monster Wurlitzer Organ played lively marches and waltzes on 255 pipes, drums, and cymbals.

Elitch's first miniature train took two years to build. It was the world's smallest passenger train. It circled the theater on twelve-inch-wide tracks. The engine belched

Know More!

Today, you can find the original Elitch's carousel at the Kit Carson County Fairgrounds in Burlington, Colorado. It still costs just 25 cents to ride. Find out more at this website: http://www.kitcarsoncountycarousel.com/about.html. You can even listen online to tunes played on the Monster Wurlitzer Organ. Close your eyes and imagine riding the carousel on a beautiful summer's afternoon a hundred years ago.

Courtesy Jack Olson/Kit Carson County Carousel Association.

Elitch's first carousel was one of the fastest in the country. It took riders' breath away, twirling them round the platform at twelve miles per hour.

From *Experiences of the Only Woman ... to Manage a Zoo.* Courtesy, Denver Public Library

Mary often joined children on Elitch's miniature train. Here she's wearing a hat and sitting at the end of the train.

steam and spat hot sparks. The eight cars were just forty-two inches long and fourteen inches wide. Each carried three to four children or two skinny adults. The tiny train worked hard. On a record day, 15,000 passengers rode the miniature train!

Thomas Long was more interested in the gardens than in rides and amusements. He designed new flower beds and worked in Elitch's **greenhouses**. He grew plants not only to plant on the grounds, but also to sell to other people for landscaping. In 1912, he was appointed to the Denver parks board. He became a well-known expert on park and landscape design.

Meanwhile, Mary imagined bigger and better attractions for Elitch's. She threw herself into more **ambitious** projects than ever. She replaced the original log entrance gate. Angels decorating a grand, Greek-style entrance now welcomed visitors.

In 1914, Elitch's opened what was called a "dark ride." The Old Mill Tunnel of Love took couples on a slow boat trip along an enclosed canal. Sweethearts floated past lighted scenes from fairytales such as "Cinderella." Many a first kiss was stolen on this ride.

One of Mary's most expensive and elaborate projects opened in 1910. She built a new theater to stage a famous naval battle. The *Monitor* and the *Merrimac* had clashed on the high seas in America's Civil War. Full-sized models of the ships re-created the battle for astonished audiences. The mechanical and electrical special effects were awesome for their time. When the theater burned to the ground four years later, it was a great loss to Elitch's.

By far, the Battle of the Monitor and Merrimac *was the biggest attraction ever at Elitch Gardens. The huge building makes the people entering look tiny.*

Mary lived for Tuesdays. Each summer, Tuesday was Children's Day. Children came to play in the Gardens for free. Parents knew their sons and daughters would be safe and happy when they dropped them off at Elitch's gate for the day.

Mary organized classes in folk dance and ballet, drama and music. Children studied plants and animals with real live examples. She offered arts and crafts, games, and contests. Always, she joined in the fun.

Though she had none of her own, Mary's loved children. They naturally loved her in return. Denver poet James Brown Adams described Mary's special relationship with them in this verse:

O, bright the ripplings of laughter, the shoutings of innocent glee,
And sunny the sweet little faces for the day from home discipline free;
'Tis a glowing of fairyland centered in the shade of the trees and the bowers,
On Children's Day out at the Gardens, with the wee ones, the birds and the flowers.

Her smile to them is a sunbeam, soft shed from the heavens above.
They cling to her hands and her skirtings with trusting, sweet innocent love.
They gambol and play all about her, and think all too short are the hours
On Children's Day out at the Gardens, with their queen and the birds and the flowers.

Mary enjoyed the Gardens' weekly Children's Days as much as the boys and girls who were her guests for free activities and classes.

By the early 1900s, more than 3,000 boys and girls attended each Children's Day. Mary hired assistants to help her look after them all. Not a single child was ever hurt in an accident. But one little girl had a close call. She ran ahead of the rest of the group. They found her sitting on top of the lion's cage. She was reaching in to stroke the lion's head! The animal was used to Mary, but not to strangers. Everyone held their breath. Mary called the lion's name. She talked to him softly. Then she quickly took the little girl's hand and drew her away from danger.

A weekly newsletter, the *Children's Companion,* published upcoming events and news of the Gardens. It was popular with adults, too. Elitch's also held free days for the Old Ladies Home and for **orphanages**. It was a favorite spot for Sunday school and church groups. Family reunions found plenty of space and lots to do. Local companies large and small planned their annual employee picnics in the Gardens.

Other Denver amusement parks served alcohol. But Mary refused. She did not want to turn Elitch's into a beer garden. People who drank too much could cause trouble. Mary held her park to high standards of safety, quality, and good taste. Elitch's visitors counted on clean, wholesome fun at her park.

As time went on, Mary and Thomas drifted apart. He concentrated on his park planning and landscaping interests. She focused on entertainment and making people happy. They seemed to be working at cross purposes. They both began to **neglect** the day-to-day details of running the Gardens. Once a fine businesswoman, Mary let some things slide as she grew older. Along with the laughter and the scent of flowers, a change was in the air at Elitch's.

5 Business and Pleasure

Have you ever heard someone described as "generous to a fault?" It means they give away too much for their own good. That was true of Mary Elitch Long.

Mary cared more about making life better for others than she cared about making money. Besides free days, the Gardens hosted many fundraisers. On these occasions, all the money from admissions went to good causes and charities. Once, Mary's friend Maggie Brown, popularly known as the "Unsinkable Molly Brown," performed to raise money for an organization called Kindness to Animals. The famous Mrs. Brown demonstrated the yodeling skills she had learned in Switzerland.

Mary's generosity was very good for the community. But it was not very good for her business. The park owed a lot of money. Mary did not pay much attention to the problem. Investors who owned stock in the company did.

A group of stockholders sent John Mulvihill, money manager for the Denver Gas & Electric Company, to check on Elitch's accounts. Mulvihill discovered that the Longs had not been paying their bills. Even worse, they had not paid their taxes. The situation was serious. Elitch's would have to be sold in order to pay back the money the Longs owed.

It did not take long to find a buyer. The Sells-Flotto Circus offered to buy the Gardens. They intended to turn the grounds into a winter home for their circus animals. They would close the park to the public.

The people of Denver did not want the new owners to change Elitch's. A group called Friends of the Gardens tried to help. They held a fundraiser for Mary at the City Auditorium. Hundreds of well-wishers came. The big show included opera, drama, ballet, symphony, and vaudeville. The event showed how many people cared about Mrs. Elitch Long and her park. But it did not raise enough money to stop the sale.

John Mulvihill bought Elitch's in 1916. As the new owner, he did not want to change the Gardens. He just wanted to be sure the business was run well. Mulvihill closed the Gardens for two seasons during World War I.

He paid all the past-due bills and back taxes. Then he set to work to make Elitch's better than ever.

Mulvihill knew that Mary herself was Elitch's most valuable **asset.** She was the heart and soul of the place. He promised her that the name of the park would never be changed. He also promised that Mary could live on the grounds for as long as she liked. And he promised that the two lower boxes in the theater would always be reserved for Mary and her friends. He wanted her to continue in her role as the **gracious** and beloved Lady of the Gardens.

Mulvihill knew a lot about money and accounting. He knew nothing about amusement parks or zoos. The business was out of Mary's hands, but the vision for the Gardens was still hers.

Together, Mulvihill and Mary kept the Gardens growing. One of the first additions under the new ownership was the Trocadero Ballroom. Mary had always frowned on public dancing. But now there was a new owner making decisions. The dance floor was bigger than a football field. The polished wooden planks were cushioned by thick horsehair pillows underneath. The ballroom featured high ceilings and fancy arches. The building style matched the carousel shell. Green and white awnings decorated the yellow stucco outer walls.

Colorado Historical Society #1003821B. Courtesy of the Gurtler Family.

Although Mary initially disapproved of adding the Trocadero Ballroom to Elitch's attractions, a more beautiful place for public dancing could not be found.

Public dancing was a very formal **pastime** in those days. Afternoon Tea Dances at "The Troc" required white gloves. Ladies carried dance cards on strings. Gentlemen wrote their names on the cards next to the type of dance they wished to share. The waltz, turkey trot, and two-step were popular. Dancers who did not mind their manners were politely tapped on the shoulder and asked to leave the floor.

In 1920, Mary became a widow for the second time. "Thomas D. Long Dies in Auto Accident on Highway near Springs" reported the September 14, 1920, *Denver Post* headline. His new motorcar crashed through a guardrail on a tight mountain curve and plunged down a steep slope. By the time other motorists reached the wreck, Long was dead. His only passenger was Mrs. Frank F. Crump who owned a Colorado Springs greenhouse that he managed. Mrs. Crump was not seriously injured.

For Mary Elitch Long, life was like a roller coaster ride. She took a deep breath, held on tight, and waited to see what happened next. Mary once said, "One must never rage and demand things, either of life or of God. Be receptive. Be ready, and everything that comes will find its place and be the best thing for you."

By this time, Elitch's first carousel was outdated. Newer "jumping" carousels had animals that moved up and down as the ride turned. Elitch's sold the original carousel to Kit Carson County for its fairgrounds. Mulvihill ordered a custom-made $20,000 jumping carousel to take its place. The new ride took three years to create. The animals were decorated with real gold and aluminum leaf. Of the 64 animals, 44 were "jumpers" and 20 were "standers." No two were alike.

In 1922, Elitch's opened the "Wildcat," a thrilling seventy-five-foot-high wooden roller coaster. "Twist his tail and hear him roar!" the ads teased. Visitors dared each other to brave the new ride. Young people especially loved it.

An automobile entrance was added. Zoo buildings were torn down to make way for a parking lot. New greenhouses protected flowers until they were ready to be planted in decorative flower beds. Expanding into the florist business was a natural next step. The Elitch-Long Floral Company delivered flowers all over town. Colorado carnations were its specialty.

Mulvihill came up with a memorable advertising **slogan:** "Not to see Elitch's is not to see Denver." It meant that Elitch's Gardens was one of the best things about the city. It was really true.

Mulvihill also built a fine stucco house in the Gardens for Mary. Her later years were filled with contentment. Beautiful trees and plants, and her animal

Know More!

Elitch's florists invented a way to color white carnations. Others had tried using powdered dyes sprinkled on the petals. The results were messy and uneven.

The Elitch's florists tried putting liquid dye in the water with cut carnations. The color soon drenched every petal.

You can do the same experiment. Put a few drops of Easter egg dye or food color into the water in a jar or vase. Add white carnations that haven't opened yet to the vase of colored water. When the flowers bloom, you should have beautiful colored blossoms.

and theater "families" surrounded her. In a wide sunhat and flowing gown, the gracious hostess continued to welcome visitors of all ages.

The theater remained Mary's greatest passion. Throughout the summer, she invited friends to share the fourteen seats in the two theater boxes reserved for her. Mary often asked twenty or more friends to join her. Ushers remembered last-minute scrambles to find enough empty seats for her many guests.

In 1925, the Denver Women's Press Club held a special birthday party for Mary. Colorado's governor and Denver's mayor congratulated her. Writers and reporters sang her praises. They thanked the Lady of the Gardens for bringing joy and beauty to their corner of the world.

John Mulvihill died in 1930. The park passed to his son-in-law, Arnold Gurtler. Gurtler had a talent for design and decoration. He made the park even more beautiful.

During the Great Depression years, many people lost their jobs. Poor, hungry families needed escape more than ever. Gurtler's ads invited them to "come to Elitch Gardens, where a quarter can buy a day of dreams."

Summer fun-seekers rarely worried about the time. But Elitch's famous Floral Clock kept track of the day,

In her later years, Mary (on the left) delighted in inviting friends to share her Elitch Theatre boxes for summer stock performances.

Colorado Historical Society, # 10038310

date, and hour. A decorative flower bed made up the face. A buried electrical motor powered the hands. Even in this magical place, time steadily ticked away.

Throughout her life, Mary Elitch Long was photographed holding flowers. The beauty and delicacy of the flowers are reflected in Mary's face.

6 The Spirit of the Gardens

As Mary grew older, she became weak and **frail**. Her health was poor. Living alone was finally too difficult for her. She had to leave her house in the Gardens. In 1932, she moved nearby to live with her sister-in-law at 4567 38th Avenue.

Moving away from Elitch's must have made life seem empty to Mary. For 40 years, the park had been her home. On July 16, 1936, Mary Elitch Long suffered a stroke. She slipped from her living room chair to the floor, unconscious. Four days later, her heart stopped. The Lady of the Gardens passed away at the age of 80.

Denver Post reporter Frances Wayne wrote in Mary's **obituary**: "The better part of her life story will not be found in books…but in the hearts and memories of those who came into contact with a personality whose quick sympathy, understanding, joyousness, gentleness, and rare good humor enriched the experience of each."

Mrs. Elitch Long's funeral was held in Denver's Cathedral of the Immaculate Conception. Her old friend Monsignor William F. O'Ryan led the memorial service. He compared Mary to Saint Francis of Assisi. "Both believed in the virtue of kindness," he said. "Both knew and understood and drew the **dumb** creatures to them, casting out fear by gentleness and the speech that is of the spirit."

In her memory, Mrs. Elitch Long's theater boxes were draped in black. The seats remained empty from the date of her death until after her funeral. Mary was buried in Denver's Fairmount Cemetery beside the great love of her life, John Elitch Jr.

Mary's handwritten will was five pages long. It listed hundreds of personal belongings. She wanted every treasured painting, book, souvenir, and knickknack given to special friends. She left many of her favorite things to children. Mary left her diamond jewelry and a pale green dress to Minnie Myrtle Mansfield Atchison. Minnie was John Elitch Jr.'s niece. Mary considered the young woman her "adopted" daughter, though she never adopted her legally.

Elitch Gardens carried on. Arnold Gurtler gave the last two elderly bears to the Denver Zoo. He filled in the old bear pit. In its place, he built a Ferris wheel.

The 1940s Big Band craze made dancing at "The Troc" more popular than ever. Swing bands from all over the country found a summer home at Elitch's. The Benny Goodman, Tommy Dorsey, and Lawrence Welk orchestras were among the most famous.

Arnold Gurtler's sons, Jack and Bud, took over management of the Gardens in 1950. They had grown up in the park. Like their father and grandfather before them, the brothers tried to honor Mary's spirit in every improvement they made.

Jack and Bud Gurtler replaced the old auto entrance with a space-age aluminum arch. Their new KiddieLand had small-scale rides just for kids. Grown-ups who sold snacks in KiddieLand booths stood in trenches, long ditches dug behind the counters. That way they could be eye-to-eye with their small customers.

The end of Mary's life is not the end of her story. She has been recognized in many ways since her death. A chair in the Central City Opera House is named for her. She was honored by both the Colorado Business Hall of Fame and the Colorado Women's Hall of Fame.

Years after she had passed on, a California man named Walt followed in Mary's footsteps. His built his amusement park not in an apple orchard, but in an orange grove. Like Mary, Walt insisted on excellence. He called his family-friendly place *Disneyland*.

Could Mary ever really leave the Gardens she so loved? Soon after her death, the spooky stories began. People reported seeing her ghost floating around the grounds. Some saw her in the theater, wearing a filmy old-fashioned gown and a large hat. The specter often spoke to, but rarely frightened, those who encountered what they believed to be her spirit.

In 1994, fourth-generation Elitch's owner Sandy Gurtler agreed to sell the amusement park business. The original Elitch Gardens closed after 104 years. Mary's dream was coming to an end. A new "Elitch's" began to rise in the central Platte River valley near downtown Denver. The next year, the new amusement park opened about six miles from the site of Mary's Gardens.

The original Gardens property was no longer miles outside of town. It was now surrounded by the city. **Developers** wanted to build houses and apartments on the grounds. Exactly sixty years and one day after Mary's death—July 17, 1996—Sandy Gurtler signed the papers for Elitch's sale. He and his wife walked the grounds for a last look around. They came across a startling sight.

Something had happened to the giant old maple tree by the theater. The trunk had been mysteriously sliced in two, five feet above the ground. There had been no wind or storm the night before. What could have caused it?

Stranger still was the way the top of the tree had fallen. It had crashed into the sturdy brick wall of an old office building. Had it fallen in the other direction, it would have hit the theater. The heavy branches would have caused a lot of damage.

Might Mary's ghost have been behind the strange tree toppling? She would have been careful not to ruin the theater. Was her spirit trying to show its unhappiness at the loss of her beloved park? Who could blame her for being upset?

"I have never spent a summer away from the Gardens, the picture I painted for all to enjoy," Mary once said. "Every tree holds its own story for me; every flower its own memory."

To this day, two reminders of the original Elitch Gardens remain on the old site. The empty carousel shell still stands, surrounded by houses and apartments. So does the playhouse, home of the longest-running

Photo by Debra B. Faulkner

Today, a small corner park on the site of the original Elitch's is dedicated to the memory of the "Lady of the Gardens." In spring and summer, the memorial stone is surrounded by the blooming plants Mary loved.

summer stock theater in America. A group of famous actresses and others raised money and fought to save the building.

More than one hundred years after it opened, the outside of the theater building was **restored**. Rebuilt, repainted, and repaired, the exterior is better than ever. Its new name is the Center for American Theatre at Historic Elitch Gardens.

Inside, the playhouse was an awful mess. Families of foxes, squirrels, mice, birds, and bats moved in when the theater closed. The spirit of animal-loving Mary herself may have invited them to take shelter there.

Workmen shooed the critters out and cleaned up after them. The leaky roof, gaps between the walls and the ground, and years of neglect caused a lot of damage to the inside of the theater. The interior will take much more work and much more money before it can open again for performances. Perhaps someday the old theater will stage a play about the remarkable life of the lady of the gardens and the joy she brought to so many people.

Timeline

1856   Mary is born on May 10 in Philadelphia, Pennsylvania

1859   Hauck family moves to San Francisco

1872   Sixteen-year-old Mary elopes with John Elitch Jr.

1880   Elitches move to Durango, Colorado

1882   Elitches move to Denver and open the Elitch Palace Dining Room

1887   John and Mary buy Chilcott Farm in west Denver

1890   Elitch Gardens and Zoological Park opens to the public on May 1

1891   John dies suddenly of pneumonia on March 10 in San Francisco

        34-year-old Mary carries on the zoo and amusement park business

1896   Elitch's shows first motion pictures in the West

1897   First season of Elitch's summer stock theater is held

1900   Mary weds Thomas D. Long

1904   Elitch's first roller coaster opens

1906   Actress Sarah Bernhardt plays Elitch Theater

        Original carousel is added

1909   Original log entrance is replaced by a stucco Greek Revival gate

1910   *Monitor* & *Merrimac* Naval Spectacle opens

1914 *Monitor* & *Merrimac* theater burns down

1916 John Mulvihill buys the Gardens

1920 Thomas Long dies in an automobile accident

Trocadero Ballroom opens for public dancing

1928 Second carousel is installed

1932 Mary moves from the Gardens to live with her sister-in-law

1936 Mary dies on July 16 at age 80

1944 Worst disaster in Elitch's history; Old Mill fire kills six people on July 16

1954 Elitch's KiddieLand opens

1958 Aluminum arch replaces stucco entrance

1975 Trocadero Ballroom is torn down

1991 The Elitch Theatre closes

1994 Original Elitch Gardens closes after 104 years

1995 New amusement park opens near downtown Denver under the Elitch name

1996 Original Elitch Gardens property is sold to developers

1998 New Elitch's becomes a Six Flags park

2006 Restoration of Elitch Theater underway

New Words

ambitious – needing a lot of work, money, or determination to succeed

amusement park – a park that charges admission and offers rides, games, and other fun things to do and see

arcade – several game booths in a row

asset – a resource important to a business

attraction – a place or thing that people want to visit or see

carousel – a circular merry-go-round ride that turns to music

convent – a house or buildings occupied by nuns

developer – a business person who buys land to build new buildings on it

dumb – unable to speak

enclosure – a closed space designed to hold something inside

frail – thin and weak

gazebo – a small, usually round, open building with a roof

gracious – warm, welcoming, and kind

greenhouse – building with clear walls and roof used to grow plants

investors – persons who put money into a business hoping to earn more back

landscaping – planting trees, shrubs and flowers in an attractive, artistic design

matinee – an afternoon theatrical performance

menagerie – a collection of animals for exhibition

neglect – to ignore or leave undone

obituary – a newspaper story written about a person's life at the time of his/her death

orphanage – a group home for children without parents or anyone to care for them

pastime – an activity done for pleasure

playwright – a person who writes plays

reputation – an opinion or knowledge about something or someone as judged by people in general

restore – to make as good as new

shares – part ownership of a business or corporation

slogan – a catchy or memorable phrase used to attract attention

sorceress – a woman who practices magic or witchcraft

vaudeville – a light-hearted variety show with several short acts

widow – a woman whose husband has died

Sources

Denver Post
Denver Republican
Denver Times
Rocky Mountain News

Denver Public Library Western History Archives – Manuscript and clippings files

Colorado Historical Society Archives – Manuscript and clippings files

Arps, Louisa Ward. *Denver in Slices: A Historical Guide to the City.* Athens: Ohio University Press, 1959.

Dier, Caroline. *The Lady of the Gardens: Mary Elitch Long.* Hollywood, CA: Hollycrofters Inc., Ltd., 1932.

Elitch, Mrs. John, Jr.. *Experiences of the Only Woman in the World Who Owns and Manages a Zoo.* Denver: [s.n., 190-?],

Elitch, Mary Hauck. *The Moth and the Moon.* Denver: [s.n., 190-?]

Fetter, Rosemary. *Colorado's Legendary Lovers.* Golden, CO: Fulcrum Publishing, 2004.

Gurtler, Jack, and Corinne Hunt. *The Elitch Garden Story: Memories of Jack Gurtler.* Boulder, Colorado: Rocky Mountain Writers Guild, 1982.

Hull, Betty Lynne. *Denver's Elitch Gardens: Spinning a Century of Dreams.* Boulder, Colorado: Johnson Books, 2003.

Leonard, Stephen J., and Thomas J. Noel. *Denver: Mining Camp to Metropolis.* Niwot: University Press of Colorado, 1990.

Varnell, Jeanne. *Women of Consequence: The Colorado Women's Hall of Fame.* Boulder, Colorado: Johnson Books, 1999.

Index

Acknowledgments

In researching this book, I discovered that the mention of Elitch's makes everyone smile. I am grateful to the many people who were delighted to help me tell Mary's story. From the beginning, Doris and Tom Baker, my publishers at Filter Press Books, were enthusiastic about adding Mrs. Elitch Long to the Now You Know Bios series. Betty Lynne Hull provided gracious and unselfish assistance with both the history of Elitch's and with historic photographs from the Gurtler family. Keith Schrum of the Colorado Historical Society (CHS) located boxes of wonderful Elitch images, and the staff of the CHS Stephen H. Hart Library patiently retrieved the files again and again as I agonized over which pictures to choose. I am grateful to the staff of the Denver Public Library Western History department for the use of their clippings files, and especially to Coi Drummond-Gehrig for helping me to share rarely seen photos from Mary's own booklet about her zoo experiences. Leona Gustafson generously provided Elitch's postcards from her collection, and the Kit Carson County Carousel Society was happy to share pictures of the historic merry-go-round they proudly preserve and operate. Thanks to my parents for taking me to Elitch's instead of Great-Aunt Lulu's, and finally to my husband, James, who is as central to my dreams as John Elitch Jr. was to Mary's.

About the Author

Historian Debra Faulkner grew up in Colorado and has fond childhood memories of summer visits to the original Elitch Gardens. Her favorite rides were the Flying Swings and the Bumper Cars.

Debra is the award-winning author of *Touching Tomorrow: The Emily Griffith Story*. She is the co-author of two books with Dr. Tom Noel – *Colorado: An Illustrated History of the Highest State* and *Colorado's Story*. She loves to bring the women of Colorado's past to life in programs. Dressed up in old-fashioned costumes, she tells their stories as though she were the historical person herself. Her students at Metropolitan State College of Denver never know who she might appear as next.